Investing

Discover The Easiest Way To Pick Stocks And Unlock
Your Financial Freedom By Investing In The Stock
Market Today

*(A Straightforward Guide To Get You Started Investing
And On The Right Track Towards Financial Independence)*

Allan Blankenship

TABLE OF CONTENT

Appreciation Is Inevitably Going To Take Place

You can get started by inquiring about the theorists' perspectives on this particular event that occurred in 2008, when the entire market experienced a decline and the economy entered a recession...

In point of fact, appreciation is likely to occur regularly over the course of a long time period. Nevertheless, for the time being, appreciation is an assumption; it is exceptional. Even if the value of the asset appreciates, there is no guarantee that it will result in a financial gain for you.

Your bottom line will be affected by some of the following factors that have

1

an effect on job appreciation: Where on the property the building is situated

A variety of urban communities each have their own distinct patterns of chronicled appreciation. Cities with dense populations, such as Los Angeles and San Francisco, are renowned for having high levels of appreciation.

It would appear that the state of California is the most important one for appreciation overall. Despite this, urban areas such as Indianapolis and Kansas City, in addition to other cities located in the Midwest, are generally recognized as being stable business sectors. This indicates that they do not typically crash as severely as other urban communities do when the economy is in a downturn, but they also do not typically crash as hard as they would otherwise like much all things considered. The third category consists of cities that are not only failing to appreciate in value but are also losing value. Through the years, the city of Detroit has served as an excellent example of this phenomenon.

The fundamentals of a city's market and the state of the economy of the surrounding area are the two most important factors that determine how much a city is worth. For example, Atlanta and Dallas were two of the most favored urban communities that emerged after the accident in 2008. However, in general, they are not known for appreciation in the same way that Los Angeles or San Francisco are known for appreciation. Despite this, Los Angeles and San Francisco were not the pioneers in appreciation during those same years as Atlanta and Dallas were.

In many cases, factors that contribute to appreciation on the market are factors. Additionally, the value of a property is not solely determined by its proximity to a significant city; rather, it is also determined by the surrounding area. Is the neighborhood located in an up-and-coming section of the larger town? Is there any kind of protection around it? Does it have good educational opportunities? Is it getting better? Although some urban communities are thought of more on a suburban-by-suburban basis in terms of great and awful neighborhoods, different urban areas like Chicago can in a very real sense change from one road to the next. In addition, the relative position of a geographic area in relation to these factors has a direct impact on the potential for appreciation.

Arrange the meeting with the landlord so that you can discuss: Despite the fact that we have touched on this stage earlier, let's go over it one again. You need to make sure that the home satisfies all of the requirements for Airbnb before you schedule a meeting with the landlord. This includes ensuring that the house is in a fantastic location, that it is being offered at an affordable price, and that it is generally suitable for Airbnb. After this, you give the proprietor a call to make arrangements for the two of you to meet in person. It was previously mentioned that you should make sure the owner, and not a delegate, is the one giving you the tour of the house so that you can present the notion of Airbnb to him.

3. Present the concept to the landlord; but, before you go to the meeting, make

sure you have everything you need to be successful. Dress nicely but not in a casual manner; there is no need to wear a student tie if you don't want to. In addition to that, make sure that you arrive there on time. When you reach to the location, you should meet up with him and shake his hand. While you are getting to know him, strike up some preliminary talk with him. You should also exchange names with him because in the long run he is not only going to be your landlord but also your business partner. For example, let's imagine he owns twenty other properties in various locations; if you join with him, you'll probably be able to acquire even more properties.

When you get there, take a walk around the property and talk to the owner by asking questions about it. This will help you get to know each other better. Be sure you are aware of how long the property has been available for rent as well as the qualifications that the landlord seeks in a renter. If you ask him, "What is the worst thing that a tenant has done?" and he responds with the horrible things that tenants have done in the past, then he has given you an advantage. In this scenario, you have asked him a question that gives you an advantage. You may then offer the landlord a solution to those problems, because it's likely that the landlord is fed up with tenants and other troubles, and if that's the case, then you're good to go. If not, then you might want to rethink your strategy. You also need to figure out what kind of landlord you're working with, as this is an important consideration. There are two distinct categories of landowners.

On the one hand, there is the sort of laid-back entrepreneur landlord who will always listen to your ideas, and on the other hand, there is the type of tense landlord who simply doesn't care and is always hesitant to try out new things and ideas. Therefore, if you find yourself in a situation with the first type of person who is more likely to agree with you, then that is the kind of person to whom you should present the proposal. Even if the landlord is the strict sort, you shouldn't rule out the possibility of renting from them. You can make your case to the strict landlord, but the vast majority of them are going to reject it. Therefore, it is essential for you to determine the type of landlord with whom you will be dealing. After getting to know the person and having a tour of the property, you should then present the concept to them. You might begin by stating something like,

"Hey, landlord! I can't tell you how much I appreciate you showing me this home. This is a good property, and I really enjoyed it, but before I go any farther, I have something important to discuss with you.

Now is the time to make your sales presentation,

"Hey, what's up with that? I think that Airbnb would be a great fit for this space. My gut tells me that this is going to be a fantastic opportunity for you to prevent tenants from wreaking havoc on your house. I am aware that as a result of using Airbnb, we will have a greater number of individuals checking in and out of the property; however, the situation is under control. We have devised a strategy that will allow us to maintain order among our guests, which includes preventing them from throwing parties and showing consideration for the property.

You continue to provide them with a lot of helpful pointers about the reasons why Airbnb is a wonderful alternative for the landlord. It's either going to be a yes or a no from him when you ask him about the concept. In the event that you receive a negative response, you will need to be prepared to address any concerns raised and possibly even make a counteroffer.

Is Participation In Video Games Necessary To Experience The Metaverse?

No. When viewed through the prism of Web3.0, the Metaverse notion involves a lot more than just videogames; yet, videogames remain an important foundation. There have been performances in Fortnite by Travis Scott and Grande Travis, and in the previous year, Lil Nas X's Roblox performance had an astounding thirty-three million views.

Companies like Stage11, which have their headquarters in Paris, are fascinating for this same reason. Stage 11 is a startup that offers metaverse-based realistic music experiences with artists such as Akon, Ne-Yo, Snoop Dogg, and David Guetta. The company has just obtained a seed investment of five million dollars from Otium Capital.

In the Metaverse, a sizeable portion of creators, ranging from musicians to fashionistas, will launch businesses centered on the provision of various services and products. Gravity Sketch has recently launched a digital collaboration space in London called Gravity Sketch, which allows designers from different locations to work together on the same three-dimensional design project.

On the more professionally oriented side of things, there are opportunities for healthcare, education, and meetings. Warping, a Swedish company that develops virtual reality training content for enterprises, has recently finished a pilot study with Kry, a virtual doctor system that allows clients who suffer from social anxiety to overcome their fears by taking part in interactive digital social environments with a trained professional.

In addition, Nvidia'sOmniverse is a part of a metaverse, and it is now creating a digital copy of a BMW manufacturing plant. Even if it's a very boring metaverse, the fact that experts can interact with it makes it all the more significant.

There are occasions when humans are taught how to lift items through the use of the Metaverse.

There are currently a great number of businesses operating in the metaverse economy, ranging from start-up ventures to multinational information technology corporations.

Virtual reality is discussed in 7.

The cutting-edge technology known as virtual reality, or VR for short, is capable of generating the impression that the user is participating in real-life activities.

Virtual reality (VR) is a type of virtual reality that is generated on a computer and in which the user is immersed while wearing a viewer. The viewer is fitted with sensors that are able to recognize the movements carried out in reality and replicate them in the digital environment.

The mind is aware that it is a work of fiction, but the senses do not pay attention to it; they believe, even if only momentarily, in what they see, hear, and touch, which results in an extremely high level of immersion.

Virtual reality can be used for a variety of purposes, including instruction and education, product design, marketing and communication, architectural visualization, and even entertainment. People who put on viewers have the ability to be transferred to a world that was created at the table, be immersed in any circumstance, train anywhere in the world without having to move, in a perfectly safe environment, and without the need for the physical presence of a trainer. People also have the ability to train anywhere in the world without having to move at all. whenever they choose, or they can work together on a project without ever having to leave their house. You can go over everything as many times as necessary until you have completely internalized everything.

You've probably been hearing a lot about virtual reality and the various applications that could be made for it recently. On the other hand, you still haven't grasped the fundamentals of this technology, such as how it works behind the scenes to let you explore virtual worlds that have a "real" feel to them. Are you interested in acquiring further knowledge on this subject, then? Yup? Very nice! Make sure you are comfortable, spend as much time as you need to concentrate on reading the following paragraphs, and you will see that by the time you have finished this in-depth look at the topic, you will have a better understanding of how virtual reality functions.

First things first, let's have a look at what virtual reality actually is: As I

17

mentioned earlier in the introduction, virtual reality (VR) is a type of simulated reality technology that is based on a three-dimensional environment that is either created on a computer or captured with lenses that are capable of showing the scene in 360 degrees. This environment can be explored by the user with the help of appropriate devices, such as visors, earphones, and gloves or controllers, among other things.

Because of this, it is evident that virtual reality results from the combination of software and hardware devices. These technologies, when used together, enable us to duplicate a virtual universe inside which the user is free to move around as if they were in a "real" setting.

The viewer and the software that is used for this purpose keep track of the user's head and body movements (I'll explain how later), changing the viewpoint and the view to your position in order to give you a relatively realistic experience. This is accomplished by keeping track of the user's head and body motions using a tracking system.

Augmented reality, often known as AR and frequently abbreviated as such, is not to be confused with virtual reality. Augmented reality, on the other hand, improves one's view of the real world that surrounds them. Apps that let you visually "wear" clothes or arrange furniture in a space before purchasing it are excellent illustrations of augmented reality.

Because of the immersive nature of virtual reality, the user is cut off from the environment that is all around him and is instead transported into a three-dimensional space that completely consumes him in all aspects. I'm hoping that you've got a good grasp on the major distinction between virtual reality and augmented reality now.

The moment has come to get a proper understanding of how virtual reality functions. As I've already indicated, the way that this technology operates is by utilizing a variety of tools, both hardware and software, which, when combined, provide the user the ability to completely submerge themselves in a virtual environment that may be very lifelike.

Several different technologies, including as head tracking, are utilized so that the experience can be made to feel as authentic as feasible. This technology allows the viewer to determine the scene to be viewed by detecting the user's direction of travel as well as head motions while they are wearing the virtual reality headset.

There are essentially two types of head tracking: one that is based on orientation, which simply detects the direction of the rotations of the user's head (for example, from left to right or top to bottom), and one that is based on position, which, instead, detects the movements of the head, associating them also with the movements made by the body, detecting movements such as the swaying of the torso forward or backward.

Opportunities For Investments In Alternative Markets

You might be in possession of a few resources that can provide you with money in the form of transactions or the gradual development of resources over time.

Some of them have the potential to be an offbeat opportunity, while others have the potential to be transformed into a source of extremely stable income.

This may be accomplished for a number of reasons, including the fact that their value increases with the passage of time, the fact that they are rare, or the possibility that you have come across a buyer who is willing to pay you a considerable amount of money for what you now possess.

They can be resources that you can sell for a profit, or they might be resources that you should keep for the long term because their value will increase with time.

First, let's take a look at the types that are the most well-known.

Objects of the past Additionally, Collectibles

Due to the fact that they are not affected by growth rates or the stock market, speculating with antiques and collectibles typically results in a higher return.

The value of collections and collectibles does not fluctuate; rather, it increases in direct proportion to the rarity and quality of the item being collected.

They have the potential to deliver extraordinary profits over a longer period of time. You should seek the recommendations of professionals or cultivate a broad knowledge base.

Clocks, currencies, cameras, comic books, stamps, bourbon, and load up games are just few of the collectibles that are considered to be among the most valuable and valuable collectibles.

According to the website sammydvintage.com, a Pinner Qing Dynasty container has a value of $80.2 million. This makes it one of the most valuable collectibles in the world.

The first step in differentiating and appreciating collectibles and collectibles is frequently determining the thing's creator by looking for an imprint or signature on the item. This can be a time-consuming process.

When it comes to identifying historic furniture, one of the most important things to look at is the era in which it was made.

The original thing was changed as little as possible, which drives up the value of the finished product.

Old fashioned sales is an excellent place to go if you need to get collectibles valued since they have experienced valuers, and as long as you carry the object with you or provide images, they will typically offer you a free valuation with the assumption that you will sell your things through them. If you need to get collectibles valued, you should go there.

The age of an item is what differentiates it as collectible, vintage, or both. Things that are considered antique typically have a minimum age of one hundred years.

Advantages include the following: • You can collect anything for investment purposes • The rarest things appreciate over the longer term • They are tangible • They can be portable • Global investments • Gain capital worth over the normal pace of inflation • You can partake in your investment • High-quality products • Stylish Disadvantages include the following: • The antique market isn't regulated • If you really want to recover the money restricted in your speculation, there are no liquid markets for antiques.

You can find collectibles and collectibles in stores, on the internet, and even in trades. Bartering is another option. You are able to sell them via the internet.

The current conditions, which included a foreclosure sale that was scheduled to take place the day after tomorrow, were the ultimate result of years of efforts to arrange a quick deal. Sam, the financial supporter who had been aggressively working the record, was on the phone with the borrower, Henry, and his dispossession guard lawyer to settle the arrangement for the following day. The following day was going to be the day that Henry would be evicted from his home. Henry made sure that everyone understood what he meant when he said to Sam, "Assuming you can get the property at a value you like at the sale tomorrow, my lawyer will not document anything to attempt to switch the abandonment deal." But if you don't buy it, then we're going to try to file anything that might stop the foreclosure sale from going through. " It appeared that everyone was on the same page, including Henry's attorney, who agreed with what was being said.

Sam had already amassed a lifetime's worth of expertise and had witnessed some truly remarkable manoeuvres that abandonment protection lawyers had done to delay a dispossession. Regardless of this fact, in all of his years working in this industry, he had never before heard of an abandonment arrangement being renegotiated after the sale. When the infamous hammer was finally laid down, in each and every instance, in his previous work, that marked the decisive turning point. Sam did not give the borrower or his lawyer any thought; however, he did focus his mental attention on the highest possible amount that he would be willing to bid on, assuming that all other factors remained same.

Upon the arrival of the agreement, Sam was in a position that was noticeably superior to that of the majority of the other dispossession closeout bidders. In light of the fact that he had been negotiating a short sale on the property before to its abandonment, he had ordered a fresh study as well as an investigation. Sam was so different from everyone else who might have been offering "with no guarantees and without having seen anything beforehand," because he was already familiar with the situation he was getting himself involved with before he ever showed up.

When the offering got underway, the primary bidders were him and a representative of the bank who needed to guarantee that the bank got their hold sum. The bid started to rise with each additional addition of $1,000. Sam had the intention of not going any higher than $375,000, but fortunately (or unfortunately), the bank delegate concluded his offering at $374,000, which meant that Sam was able to acquire the property in a practical sense at the particular highest amount he was able to pay for it. It was almost unfathomable how things could have gone down in that manner.

Sam made a beeline for the nearest bank branch and requested a clerk's cheque to cover the amount of money that was outstanding. After handing over the cash to the abandonment sell off processor, he discovered that the title to the property did not immediately become available to him. Inquisitive, he inquired as to what the break-in was since he believed that once the money was handed over, the property would be legally considered his. The worker for the public administration said, "In this state, there is a multi day time span by which, in the event that the abandonment closeout is challenged, you may not turn into the proprietor, but in any case, your cash would be returned to you." As soon as he was aware of this information, he called Henry to inform him that he had won the sale for a price that he was content with, and that taking into account what had been discussed previously, this indicated that the arrangement was now complete. Henry thanked Sam for everything he had done to try to close a deal quickly, and he was pleased to see that Sam was being compensated for all of the work he had put in by acquiring the property for the price he desired. Henry thanked Sam for everything he had done.

On the seventh day, Sam inquired about the further phases on ending his obligation for the property. Unbelievably, the record revealed that a customary report had been created by the borrower to contest the abandonment of the property. Sam was stunned by this information. Because of this, Sam would not be able to acquire the title to the property on that particular day.

Sam felt double-crossed. He immediately dialled Henry's number and asked for clarification, but all Henry could tell him was that he had shifted his perspective and that he and his attorney believed Sam had undervalued the property. This was all the information that Henry was able to provide. Sam was seething with rage.

Back on the phone with the abandoning office, he questioned, "Indeed, I surmise assuming that I won't get this property, I will get a discount of the $375,000 cash I paid you. Will that be the case?" I was wondering if it was possible for me to obtain that today. The response that was given to that question was "No. It is necessary for the adjudicator to make a request for a discount in order to receive one. The occurrence of such circumstances is exceedingly unlikely, yet it is possible that some time will pass before it does happen, if not even longer.

Not only had Sam NOT become the proprietor of that property at the acquire cost of $375,000, but in addition, that cash was currently under the guardianship of the neighbourhood government, and there was no time period on when it was going to come back!

Sam, in an alarm state, contacted a few other abandoning lawyers in order to gain a better understanding of the situation. They all responded that it was one of the many hazards in purchasing at an abandonment sell off, and furthermore that they never urged their consumers to purchase at a dispossession closeout for this and many other reasons. What's more, it's unfortunate that they all responded that it was one of the many dangers in purchasing at an abandonment sell off. Also, just when he thought things couldn't get much worse, he discovered that the local government had a severe shortage of judges, which meant that instances of abandonment were allowed to continue for an extremely extended period of time. The truth of the matter is that an arbitrator from yet another region of the state had been recruited to assist with the build-up; but, she was on a leave of absence for the next month!

An assigned authority finally provided the request to discount Sam's cash after he had been making efforts towards this goal for half a year. However, they made several mistakes on the documentation, which caused the process to be delayed by another month. At the end of the seventh month, the money was handed back. Nothing of interest There is no attempt at making peace. There is no recovery of the risk costs incurred as a result of not having that funds available to pursue alternative arrangements. In the meantime, the borrower regained ownership of the property and, thanks to a legitimate escape clause, still legally owns it today, despite the fact that the house loan isn't being paid as agreed.

Taking Advice From Everyone In Your Environment

Have I mentioned that there is a very large number of people speaking their minds out there? Not only is it possible that paying attention to everyone around you will cause you to lose your mental stability, but it's also likely that you will eventually take on some pretty horrible guidance if you do so.

I am unable to comment on whether or not you have noticed this, but the people who are close to us will frequently have a great deal of feelings over the lives of others. I believe that one of the many rites of passage that investors must go through is to encounter a multitude of people who are intent on persuading them that being involved in real estate investing is a terrible plan.

In spite of the fact that I believe it is always a good idea to at least hear and think about all of the advice that comes your way because no one can tell which piece of advice will be the real pass to your success, I am also a huge promoter of taking into consideration the source from which the advice is coming. Because of this, I feel obligated to share with you the single most important piece of advice that has guided my actions in both the real estate and business worlds: Never take advice from someone who you wouldn't feel comfortable exchanging shoes with.[9]

My involvement in my own family while I was attempting to get into contributing was one of the best examples of using this statement to assist me with concluding who I ought to be taking exhortation from. This was one of the best examples of using this statement to help me decide who I should be taking exhortation from. My grandfather was the type of person who would always get started ahead of schedule, buckle down, save every dime he could, and make sure that everyone was safe. He put in an incredible amount of work and was quite frugal. His sister, who was also my auntie, was the complete opposite. She has freely risked her money, been a consistent financial backer, and has gone through her wealth without hesitation. Both of their strategies led to a significant increase in their financial success. When I started feeling curious about making a contribution, I brought it up to the two of them, and to my surprise, I started getting encouragement from both of them to make a contribution. The problem was that every person's advice contradicted the guidance provided by the other individuals. Who exactly was I supposed to pay attention to then?

When I compared the daily routine I needed with experience to both my father's life and my auntie's life, I noticed that my vision more strongly resembled the way in which my auntie went about things. My father's life was more structured, while my auntie's life was more free-form. Even though my father is one of the most important people in my life, I've never had to devote a significant portion of my life to working for someone else and putting away every dime I earn. Therefore, when I first started thinking about making a contribution, I paid more attention to my auntie than I did to my father. There are a million other aspects of life that require my attention, but investing is not one of them. Why? Because we've never had an occasion where we needed to trade shoes on that pitch. Despite this, I would trade shoes with my auntie, who was responsible for the contributing division. As a result of this, I came to the conclusion that it would be best for me to seek advice from the person whose shoes I needed to trade with because doing so appeared to be the most logical course of action.

When it came to my becoming a business person, for example, this remark began to play a fundamental role in my life around that time. This is just one more evidence of when it happened. During the time that I was initially interested in land contributing, which subsequently led to me starting my own firm, I met somebody during a contract meeting who was living what I considered to be the life of my dreams. This encounter was the impetus for me to start my own company. Because he ran his own business, he was free to set his own hours and could take off anytime he pleased. In addition, he was able to travel whenever he desired. He was demonstrating an approach to life and a plan that was practically identical to what I required for my own life. As a consequence of this, I always paid attention to every piece of advice he ever provided to me, and as a consequence of doing so, I was eventually driven to launch a company that would enable me to have all of the same extravagances as he did. Because I would trade shoes with him, I had to pay attention to what he was saying. One way that I could have differentiated myself from that is by soliciting advice on how best to maintain my ideal life of independence from a person who wore a suit and sat behind a desk from nine in the morning until five in the afternoon every Monday through Friday.

It wouldn't give the impression of being legitimate, would it?

Art

In light of the fact that artwork is not connected to the stock market in any manner, it is possible for its value to rise even while the market is experiencing a downturn. Despite this, artwork is considered to be an extremely illiquid asset.

If you are willing to put resources into it, consider craftsmanship contributing a medium to long term extension to your portfolio. It can take a very long time to have your speciality work sold at closeout, so if you are willing to do so, consider investing in it. Creating art is not always a risk-free endeavour. Craftsmen and the work they produce are integral to the overall style, which in turn affects resale value and return on investment.

The acquisition of art typically involves substantial additional costs, such as commissions and insurance premiums. The most significant risk is that there is always a possibility of fraud, theft, or property destruction occurring.

You need to talk things over with a craftsmanship business counsellor, and you need to jot down notes about what you like and don't like about certain things.

Investing in your own education is the single most important thing you can do to put yourself in a position to achieve any level of success.

Even a copy of a work may have some monetary value, despite the fact that original works command the highest prices for their purchase.

Putting money into handiwork isn't something that will work well for everyone. Although it is typically very satisfying, there is no guarantee that the work of craftsmanship you buy will increase in value.

The following are some of the benefits of investing money in art:

• It is a physical asset • It has an enjoyment value • It has the potential to develop in value over time • It is not exposed to fluctuations in the market • It diversifies your portfolio

The obstacle that prevents more resources from being invested in art:

There is a barrier to entrance in the form of a lack of information; the asset is not liquid; maintaining it can be challenging; there is no guarantee that its value will rise over time; forgeries occur; insurance premiums are high.

• Putting Away

• Criminals may target you as a potential victim.

You can purchase handiwork at trade shows, exhibitions, fairs devoted to the craft, or even online.

Fine jewellery

In the sense that it can be the subject of ardent speculation, jewellery possesses an invaluable quality. They will maintain their value if you purchase them from the collections of the world's most renowned designers.

The use of high-quality diamonds and precious metals in each individual item is a hallmark of superior planning and contributes to the value of the finished products.

The price of a diamond can fluctuate wildly depending on a number of factors such as the colour of the stone, buyer preference, and what others are willing to pay; nevertheless, diamonds are unaffected by inflation.

In contrast to gold, the value of precious stones is not quantified in terms of their weight in carats. The value of each stone is determined by a number of factors, including its carat weight, degree of shading, degree of lucidity, and cut.

Gold is generally considered to be a safe investment; however, precious stones frequently have a higher resale value, which gives them a higher value. Outside of the realm of jewellery, the appeal of gemstones is experiencing explosive growth.

Platinum jewels are invariably more expensive than gold because of the extraordinary and rare qualities they possess; nonetheless, a precious stone is the most expensive of them.

Prices for jewellery that dates back to particular time periods can be significantly higher. Skill in labourThe era of art deco, roughly spanning the years 1920 to 1930, is currently experiencing something of a renaissance.

After a period of time, the value of particular jewels and brands has remained mostly unchanged. Authentic examples of brands with an obvious reputation for quality include Cartier and Van Cleef&Arpels, amongst others.

The following are some of the many benefits of investing your resources in jewellery:

They are irrefutable assets; they cannot be hacked or deleted; they are transportable; and they have the following features:

Investing one's resources on jewellery comes with the following potential drawbacks:

• Price • Space Available

They are not movable assets, and they do not produce any form of income or interest.

You can get them in reputable places or even at auctions if that better suits your needs.

Brokers of Real Estate

This is the option that I'm leaning towards the most. As you are probably aware, I've been working in this industry for close to twenty years, and over a significant portion of that time, my wife Teresa and I have owned and operated a land financier here in Utah under the name Wasatch Luxury. As a result, we have a strong affinity for this facet of life, and in the following paragraphs, I will talk about some of the things I've learned about it, as well as how you may choose the best Realtor partner to work with while you're going through this process and putting together your portfolio of Lifestyle Assets.

I feel it necessary to offer you some sound advice in this situation: I am the first person to admit that I believe there is something fundamentally wrong with the real estate industry as a whole, particularly with relation to realtors. Everyone seems to talk a good game, and the majority of estate agents act as if they are experts in their field and can fix anything. Despite this, the vast majority of the time they are not experts in any field. Because of this, picking the most qualified expert to collaborate with in your team will be an exceptionally difficult task. I won't get into my rant on why I think so many specialists in today's world are so incompetent and the factors that contribute to that problem because I don't want to. However, I want you to be aware that I do believe that the business as a whole is broken, and because of that, it is very challenging to choose the appropriate people to assist us with this process.

I am here to provide assistance to you in selecting an option that is suitable for your group. It is not a good idea to have every Tom, Dick, and Harry in the world sending you properties off the MLS. You should make it a priority to identify a single knowledgeable individual in your industry with whom you can collaborate. I see people making this mistake all the time, which is that they just sign up and then say, "Send me your best properties." I am a potential investor, and I am interested in viewing the properties." You wind up with a group of specialists who know nothing about businesses, who know nothing about what you're trying to do, and who bring you listings for houses that will never qualify as a valuable lifestyle asset. This is a problem for you because it means you have to deal with them. It is a tremendous waste of both your time and the time of the specialist to waste their time in this manner.

The following is a list of things that your real estate agent should be able to do for you if you want them to. Your real estate agent is typically the first resource you consult. It is reasonable for you to anticipate that your real estate agent will have the ability to educate you about the market for vacation rentals in the region to which you will be contributing. Your representative should be able to talk to you about major experiences they've had working in specific niches and subsets of the broader market as well as the smaller, more specific company sectors. They are the local experts, and they should have the opportunity to offer some of their knowledge and experiences on the local market, the micro markets, and the places within the market.

You should have the expectation that your agent will be aware of any new opportunities that arise within their area in order to aid you in the process of building your portfolio. There is a possibility that there is an additional reason why people in the fabricated local region are looking for vacation rentals. They should be in line with those fresh opportunities so that you can get closer to the front of some of those as well as some new properties that are coming the market. In an ideal environment, all you would need to do is collaborate with professionals who have knowledge regarding vacation rental deals or receive the necessary training.

They have put in the time and effort to comprehend this market as well as what you are looking for as a short-term rental financial backer or a vacation property investor.

Your representative needs to be in order and understand the local regulations and authorising requirements of short-term vacation rentals in order to be of assistance to you. Rules for drafting and the requirements for obtaining permits are constantly updated. While we are in the process of purchasing these properties, we need to pay careful attention to the neighbourhood regulations and requirements to determine whether or not we can legally operate a short-term rental property inside that neighbourhood. Your agent needs to provide you the choice to have them assist you with that, as well as the opportunity to have them assist you in seeing some of the restrictions that you might not be aware of.

Your representative should provide you the opportunity to connect with their network of professional contacts. This should be a choice. The most of the time, their company is going to be a really active hub for off-market properties. Your representative should have an outstanding list of professional contacts that they can share with you as you begin to put together your fantasy team and put together your group of professionals who you really want to work with as you go down this road. This is something that they can do for you as you begin the process of putting together your fantasy team.

Analysis Of Stock Markets From A Fundamental Perspective

The stock market can be predicted using fundamental analysis, which involves analysing economic fundamentals and the financial soundness of companies. In addition to that, the approach keeps track of any news stories that might have an impact on the way market prices move.

The fundamental analysis is thought to be more difficult than the technical analysis since it takes into consideration a greater number of aspects. This strategy has the disadvantage that it cannot determine the points at which one should enter or leave a market. You can't also use it to figure out where to place stop loss and take profit orders, because you can't use it to do that. The procedure focuses on determining the true worth of the stock market as it currently stands. It entails the investigation of each and every facet of the market, such as the conditions of the many industries, the financial situations of the companies, and the economy as a whole. In addition to that, it takes into account earnings on stocks, assets, expenses, and liabilities.

By analysing both small cap and large cap firms, the fundamental analysis provides investors with the ability to identify stocks that are trading at an incorrect price. First, the analyst will conduct research on the economy as a whole, and then he will focus his attention on specific companies and industries in order to arrive at a price for the stock that is reasonable. This approach makes use of data that is already available to the public, such as interest rates, credit ratings, revenue, and return on equity.

In the context of fundamental analysis, a stock is considered to be undervalued when its intrinsic value is more than the price at which it is currently trading. If the stock's intrinsic worth is lower than its current market price, then the stock is overpriced. Investors make their decisions regarding whether or not to buy or sell a specific type of stock based on the information provided here. The majority of investors will buy a company at a time when they believe it is undervalued and will sell it when they believe it is expensive.

Fundamental analysis is difficult to define for a lot of people because it takes into account so many different factors that are connected to the health of the market. It is possible to classify all of the elements that go into determining a market's fundamental status into two distinct categories: qualitative variables and quantitative aspects. The factors that can be stated through the use of numbers or numerical phrases are known as quantitative factors. The characteristics that characterise the nature of something are known as its qualitative factors. These cannot be reduced to a numerical value. Quantitative factors are, to put it another way, those that are represented by cold, hard figures. These are the observable characteristics of any industry or company, and they supply the bulk of the information that is included in financial statements. The qualitative factors are not able to be touched. They stand for a variety of things, including a company's recognition, propriety, and leadership excellence, amongst many other things.

When determining market pricing, analysts often take into consideration four primary qualitative elements. These include:

The business model of a corporation is comprised of its values, mission, and vision statements. It explains why a firm even exists and how it conducts its business.

Advantage concurrent with competitors One definition of a company's competitive advantage is its capacity to continue to maintain its position at the top of its industry. The majority of businesses that enjoy a significant edge in the marketplace see increased profits as a result of their stock listing. Better dividends, trading environments, and stock prices are something that the shareholders of such companies can always look forward to enjoying.

Leadership is one of the variables that will define the success of a firm, and it is one of the most important factors. How strategic a company's leadership or management is directly correlates to how powerful the company will become. If the leaders of a company don't believe in the reason for the company's existence, it doesn't matter how good their business plan is; the company could still fail. Even if it can be difficult for you to analyse the leadership of a company before purchasing shares from it, you can still look at the company website to get a general understanding of how the company is organised. You have the opportunity to gather more information about the leaders, including how effectively they performed in their past roles.

Governance is a term that refers to the policies and procedures that a corporation has in place. These frequently represent the relationship that exists between an organisation and the people who have a stake in it. You need to make sure that the company you invest in is operated fairly and with at least some amount of openness before you put your money into it, and fundamental analysis helps make sure that you understand this.

The market share, consumer base, regulations, and competition are some of the additional characteristics that fall under this group. In one way or another, each of these elements has an effect on the state of a company's finances. This will ultimately result in either an increase or a decrease in the price of the stock in the future.

Quantitative aspects are primarily represented in the financial accounts of an organisation, as was previously noted. These values have an effect on the financial performance of the company. The balance sheet, the income statement, and the cash flow statement are the three most crucial statements that are utilised in the process of performing a financial analysis.

A company's balance sheet is a record that details its equity, assets, and obligations at a given point in time. The equation that is used to get a balance for these is as follows:

Assets equal Liabilities plus Equity.

A company's assets are the resources that it owns at a particular point in time. They consist of things like machinery, buildings, currency, and inventories. A company's debts are referred to as its liabilities, while the amount of money an owner has personally put in a company is referred to as the equity of that company.

The performance of a particular business during a specific time period is reflected in the income statement of that business. It includes information such as profits, revenues, and expenses, among other things.

Cash flows are a measure of how money enters and exiting the organisation has changed over time. This encompasses monies received not only from operating the firm but also from investing and financing it. The term "cash from investing" refers to any money that was placed into the assets of the firm, in addition to earnings gained from the sale of other enterprises or assets. The money that is paid for or received as a result of borrowing or lending money is referred to as cash from financing. Cash flow from operations refers to the money earned by a company via its regular business activities.

The majority of financial markets make use of two primary concepts: the technical analysis and the fundamental analysis. Despite the fact that their functions are practically identical, there is a significant difference between them. While fundamental analysis examines the market from a more in-depth perspective, technical analysis examines how current market activity might be used to predict future trends. A fundamental analyst, for instance, won't rely on charts to forecast future market movements; rather, he or she will seek an understanding of how these charts were developed and the ways in which they can influence the stock's inherent worth. The following table provides an overview of the further distinctions that exist between these two ideas.

Different Types Of Mutual Funds

There are four primary groups or categories of mutual funds to choose from. The first category of mutual fund invests in individual companies' shares of stock. These are also referred to as equity funds at times. There are a few distinct types of mutual funds that fall under this category. These types are typically differentiated by the objective of the investments they pursue. For instance, if you are primarily interested in receiving dividends, you will most likely find an equity fund that also pays out income to be of great interest to you. This is going to be a mutual fund that invests in a big number of equities that pay dividends, and after that, the fund is going to divide up the dividends and distribute them on a per-share basis. This determination is made based on the total number of shares or units in the mutual fund. Therefore, the fund will receive the dividend payments from all of the stocks that it owns, and after that, it will divide the total amount of those payments among the whole number of shares that are held in the mutual fund. Following that, you will get payment in an amount that is equivalent to the number of shares you already possess.

In addition to growth funds and sector funds, there are also sector funds accessible. As was said above, a substantial number of prominent mutual funds also replicate the performance of important stock indices, such as the S&P

500. A greater proportion than half of all mutual funds are invested in equities.

You might also put your money into mutual funds that invest in fixed-income securities. This is not to be confused with income funds, which are investments that are made up of equities that pay dividends. Bonds are the asset class that mutual funds referred to as fixed-income funds invest in. These can vary greatly from one another due to the fact that certain bond funds will concentrate on government bonds while others will concentrate on corporate bonds as their primary investment objective. Bonds are essentially loans made by investors to a government or corporation, despite the fact that most people do not consider bonds to be loans; rather, they consider bonds to be investments. A bond, therefore, functions in the same manner as a traditional loan in that it requires interest payments and has a maturity date at which the principal amount is repaid. In contrast to the kinds of loans that a person may apply for, the organisation or government entity is solely responsible for making interest payments; they do not make scheduled payments on the principal; rather, they hold onto it until the end of the bond's tenure.

Investments in stocks are made by aggressive growth funds, although the emphasis is placed on fast expanding small size companies and new ventures. Some aggressive growth funds also invest in emerging companies in developing countries that have a strong potential for significant amounts of growth. These markets are known as "high-potential" markets. These funds are considered to carry a high level of risk. They are also capable of experiencing significant declines in proportion to their overall growth.

There is also a type of mutual fund known as "balanced funds" that allows investors to assemble their portfolios according to a variety of criteria in order to achieve their financial objectives. Some of the money in balanced funds will be invested in stocks, some of it will be invested in bonds, and some of it will be invested in various other sorts of financial securities.

Funds that invest in money markets are the last option. These are investments with a very low level of risk, with a primary focus on low-risk bonds such as U.S. treasuries.

Do It Yourself Investment Portfolio

When you begin researching ETFs to include in your portfolio, you will quickly realise that there are hundreds of options available. This is something that you may already be aware of. Before beginning your search, I would suggest that you become very concentrated; in other words, you should know exactly what it is that you desire.

"I want an investment portfolio with a lot of equity exposure..." is not sufficiently specific. It is not sufficient in any way.

The following is an example of how your list of investment requirements should look:

70% of the total ownership

Bond allocation at a rate of 30%

ETFs based in Ireland have the industry's lowest management fees and only trade in USD.

This is a feasible and extremely laser-focused strategy. But give the following exercise a shot if you haven't settled on the level of danger you're willing to take.

Meditation with Guided Imagery: Risk and Uncertainty Evaluation of One's Capacity for Tolerance

Putting together an investment portfolio is comparable to working with putty.

According to the perspective of one investor, a portfolio that is composed of 60% shares and 40% bonds is a "aggressive portfolio" because it has a high share proportion. To a different investor, this portfolio might look like a secure and comfortable one that would be acceptable for use as a retirement plan.

Let's put this example of a 60/40 portfolio to work for us and try this exercise:

Close your eyes and picture the following scenario when you are trying to decide what kind of assets should be included in the investment portfolio you have created for yourself:

The time now is 7:15. You are still quite fatigued, and you find that you are unable to keep your eyes open. You force yourself to go into the kitchen, where you prepare a cup of black coffee. While you are waiting for it to brew, you decide to check Facebook, and to your astonishment, you discover that there is a brand new financial crisis on the horizon. You click on a new tab on your browser and go straight to logging into your investment portfolio. You smack the table with your hand, spilling your cup of coffee. Your hands are trembling just little. Your stock just experienced a fifty percent loss in value.

Now you need to ask yourself: what number, if it were shown to you in red, would prevent you from getting a good night's sleep?

If the value of your investment portfolio was $150,000:

ETFs that invest in global equities make about sixty percent.

40% of the portfolio is invested in a global bond ETF.

The figure that is glaring at you in crimson the morning in question is now $45,000, and it is shown in a brilliant red.

Don't forget that this is just an example; the loss is only theoretical as long as you haven't actually parted with any of your possessions. However, the very idea of it still gives me the creeps. Even for the lazy investor who has read this book and already knows that international events that affect bouncing stock indices are immaterial, this is a dreadful time since the lazy investor won't be able to cash in that investment for another 35 years!

However, the pain is still significant, particularly if this is your first time dealing with a catastrophe of this magnitude on a worldwide scale. At the end of the day, it doesn't matter how well you can control your feelings; you're still a human being. The way in which one reacts to a falling market is very similar to how one reacts after suffering a loss.

The emotions are quite real. Nevertheless, we are the only ones who can be held accountable for our actions. Will this morning's cataclysmic events terrify you to the point that you will hit the "SELL" button on your trading platform only to prevent further potential losses? Are you going to act rashly and emotionally, forgetting the "leave it alone" strategy that you set up for yourself?

Again, you should close your eyes and picture yourself suffering a loss of fifty percent of the stocks in your portfolio. Think of the numbers as they actually are. How does one react to that? Terrible, right? Is it manageable? Or perhaps you still consider yourself to be a robot and say to yourself, "Whatever! I have another 35 years of service left in me! The market has experienced drops in the past, and it will eventually recover...just like it did before!

Any and all sentiments are acceptable, to be expected, and part of the natural human experience. Congratulations are in order if the notion of the defeat made your spine tingle. You are not in the appropriate exposure range, and you need to lower the stock share in your portfolio to a level that will allow you to continue sleeping soundly even in the midst of a financial crisis. During the stock market crisis that was caused by COVID-19, holders of investment portfolios that contained significant amounts of shareholdings saw their holdings suffer a significant decrease.

The S&P 500 index saw a one-day decline of 12% on March 16, 2020. A lot of people were alarmed when they saw terrifying figures in bright red in their financial portfolios.

In the space of only a few short days, my personal investment portfolio suffered losses that were roughly equal to several salaries' worth of income. However, I did not find that taking a sleeping medication or listening to lullabies helped me get a good night's rest. Ignorance was the key to my peaceful nights; it didn't take much of it. I was blissfully ignorant about everything and everything having to do with finances. Even though I heard rumours about the stock markets falling, just like everyone else who was listening to the news, I didn't rush to my computer to check my investment portfolio because of the news. Sure, I heard those rumours, just like everyone else who was listening to the news. Why? My interest was not piqued.

Losses are considered theoretical and most likely transient as long as the investments in question have not been sold. Because I was investing for the long term — decades — I wasn't interested in how much the stock market fell on March 16, 2020, and I wasn't interested in how much it fell or increased on any other day in 2020, either. I was investing for the long term, so I didn't care if it rose or sank. At the very earliest, I won't require this money until the year 2050!

This complacent investor was not frightened by the COVID-19 issue because I felt that mankind will get through it just as it had gotten through past global crises that came before it. Will a year pass as we wait? Perhaps five years from now? It makes no difference. I have a reasonable degree of optimism that by the year 2050, all of current economic panic will have passed. It was a pleasant surprise to find out that, in terms of the stock market, humanity healed faster than a Hollywood-conscious uncoupling — precisely three and a half months.

Getting The Most Out Of Your Financial Reserves

You probably already know that having a budget will enable you to put money away so that you can eventually attain the goals that are truly important to you in the future. It increases your wealth without depriving you of anything at the same time. If saving money has such significant advantages, why is it so difficult for the majority of people to do it?

Because most individuals want everything right now, saving money can be a challenge for most of them. You can get practically whatever you desire, but it won't be available right now. Have you ever seen how babies react when they aren't given a bottle right away? They start to wail. Even older children and adults are becoming giddy about the prospect of purchasing new goods right now. If you can improve how you feel about having to wait for what you want, you will be able to save more money and buy better items in the future.

How to simplify the process of monetary cost cutting

As soon as you get some money, put some of it in savings. Put it away in a safe location like a drawer or a pig bank. Labelling envelopes, folders, or jars with labels such as "Long Term," "Short Term," "Gifts," "Savings," "Charity," or any other label that may be significant to you is another wonderful strategy for saving money and putting money aside for certain goals.

Comparison shopping for different interest rates

If you start saving at a younger age, for example, your money will have grown by a greater amount by the time you reach the age of twenty-one. There are some banks that will provide you interest on your money if you maintain it in their accounts. They make an offer to you on an annual basis for a share of the money that you maintain in their bank. The term "interest" refers to this proportional amount. Keep in mind that you are the bank's customer whenever you visit the institution. You shouldn't be shy about asking inquiries because the bank is interested in having your business. They are under the impression that if you begin using their banking services while you are young, you will continue to do business with them even as you get older and demand more sophisticated financial assistance. You have a lot of power for someone at such a young age thanks to this!

Think about how your money can increase if you start saving when you're young. The following is an illustration of how much more money you will have at age twenty-one if you invest one thousand dollars in a bank account and receive the standard amount of interest each year.

Your beginning age is now if you make a yearly deposit of one thousand dollars:

Because interest is always expressed as a percentage, as you can see, a five percent interest rate indicates that you will earn five cents for every $1 that you lend to the bank (or deposit there). Your interest may be credited to your account on a monthly, semiannual, or annual basis, depending on the bank or other lender that you work with.

The most beneficial course of action for you would be to arrange to have interest added to your account on a regular basis. Why? Compounding is the process that determines whether or not your interest earns additional interest, and it is this process that determines how quickly the interest accumulates. That means the money you've already earned is now generating additional revenue for you to use!

Start putting money away as soon as you can. You can see for yourself that the better off you will be in the long run, the higher the interest rate. As a consequence of this, you need to do some comparison shopping in order to find the greatest bargain. The operation is as follows:

Make sure you ask your financial institution how often interest is added to your account.

Request a graphic that displays the different pricing options they offer.

Find out whether they offer discounts to customers with smaller accounts.

Investigate whether or not they take an interest in the holidays.

Find out whether you can still collect interest on the money you withdraw before the end of the year if you do so before the end of the year. whether you do so, find out if you can still collect interest on the money you withdraw. This practise is known as crediting from the day of the deposit to the day of the withdrawal.

Find out whether the bank will charge you a fee if you don't make regular deposits of money into your account.

Determine whether you are able to access your account online through the bank's website at no cost to you or whether you are required to pay a fee to do so.

Check to see if there are any additional costs involved with maintaining the account.

Find a point of entry: Once you have determined when you are going to want to get while the getting is good, the following step is to determine when you are going to want to jump in on a profitable option trade in general. This may be done by determining when you are going to want to get while the getting is good. To accomplish this goal in the most effective manner, you should begin by determining the maximum level of risk that you are willing to take, and then, once you have identified a course of action that is consistent with that level of risk, you should select what action you wish to take next. The choice to purchase a single option is by far the most typical way to enter the market. You are also going to want to take into consideration secondary factors, and the extent to which you do so will depend on the level of risk you are willing to take. This is because you want your entrance point to be selective enough to weed out poor propositions, but not so severe that even the good ones are unable to get through. The more experience you have trading options, the simpler it will be to identify the optimal point at which to enter a trade.

Inquire within regarding your objectives: It is important to have a distinct understanding of just what you expect to accomplish when it comes to long term trading so that you then have a better idea of how each individual trade may help you move one small step closer to your goals. When it comes to building the type of trading system that is suitable for you, it is vital to have a clear idea of just what you hope to accomplish when it comes to long term trading. When it comes to defining your goals, you want to make sure that you take into account any restricting constraints, but at the same time, you want to make sure that your goals are both realistic and what is known as SMART.

S: The most effective goals are those that are detailed in the sense that they make it crystal obvious why it is that you want to achieve the goal in question as well as which needs stand in the way of your accomplishment. It will also make it apparent when the objective is likely to be achieved, where the completion will take place, and who you will need to call upon in addition to yourself in order to effectively complete it. It is critical to have specific goals since they significantly increase the likelihood that the goals will be achieved in comparison to more general ones.

The best goals are measurable, which means they contain numerous points that can provide unique feedback as to the overall success or failure of the goal as a whole. M: The best goals are quantifiable. M: The best goals are measurable. Your goal is quantifiable if you are able to determine with absolute certainty when you have moved on to the next stage.

A: You will have the most success in achieving your goals if you take into account all of the specific difficulties you face. No matter how excellent your intentions are, setting a goal that is impossible to achieve is never a good idea.

R: The most effective objectives are those that are practical, which indicates that they are not only attainable but also capable of being accomplished depending on the amount of time and work that you are going to be able to put forth on average.

Timely: The best goals are those that have a definite timeline for fulfilment that is not only reasonable, but also very detailed. When it comes to a timeline, goals that are too specific will never be accomplished in the allotted time; on the other hand, goals that are too open-ended will also never be accomplished because it will be too simple to put them off indefinitely. Neither scenario will ever result in the desired level of success.

Maintain a record of your accomplishments: It is highly likely that you will find it helpful to keep extremely detailed notes regarding the trades you have made, the mental state you were in when you made them, and the ultimate outcome of each deal. This is especially true if you are just starting out in the world of options trading. It is essential that you monitor these metrics all throughout your day, each and every day; nevertheless, you should make it a point not to obsess over them at the conclusion of each day with the intention of making a decision regarding your system. A decent system requires at least a few weeks to decide if it is worthwhile at all, and then another two weeks to determine if its outcomes are near or above 50 percent. There is no benefit to be gained from searching for results where there are none that are significant enough to be viewed accurately. If you can exercise some patience, the information you need to analyse will prove to be lot more helpful.

How To Recognize Winning Penny Stocks Before The Market Strike

What aspects of a penny or microcap firm should investors prioritise when making their selection? When it comes to investing in penny stocks, there is a set of guidelines that you should follow and make sure to keep in mind.

Find the stocks that you can plainly see are on the verge of making big gains. One of the quickest methods to determine this is to locate a stock that is already moving in the desired direction. This is typically observable through the use of charts and several other types of analysis. It is important to keep in mind that due to information inefficiencies, it may be impossible to catch it from the beginning, but this does not imply that you cannot hop along while it is still a part of the move.

Always be on the lookout for potential breakouts that have the ability to reach new highs. A beneficial approach that one should be aware of is looking for a stock that has the potential to achieve new highs, particularly during the trading day. For instance, if you notice that it is truly the afternoon of a Friday and the stock price is still maintaining the same high as it was in the morning, there is always the possibility of a short squeeze occurring before the market shuts. A short squeeze is something that every penny stock trader absolutely needs to educate themselves on how to recognise in the marketing world since it has the potential to be profitable for them in the long term. This is due to the fact that when possible breakouts do happen to hit the new highs, they will not be able to retain the price in their previous resistance level. As a result, in the end, you will be generating bigger gains than ever potentially could have been predicted.

One further piece of advice to follow to the letter is to ensure that you are always betting the price on the action. The way prices have been moving over time tells you a pretty accurate tale about what's going on with the stock. Companies can be dishonest, but the data and statistics don't lie. Even if none of the news websites in the world provide any indication of what is taking place, it is possible to determine whether a stock is reaching a new high or beginning a downward trend on your own. You should put your complete attention and capacity towards utilisingthe stock charts because they are a significant and relevant information instrument.

Take your time and keep an eye on how prices are moving. Even if nothing else, it will prove to be educational, and despite the fact that it may prove to be very monotonous, this is the best method to pick up on trends that you almost likely would not have noticed otherwise. Create some interest in the situation by making it into a game. Put your money where your mouth is by placing bets on the stock price you think will go next. If you are incorrect, you should investigate the reason for your error; however, if you are correct, you should feel free to congratulate yourself with an excellent cup of coffee or tea. You most surely were deserving of it!

Once you feel like you have a better handle on your betting game, you might want to think about putting money into your predictions. If you don't feel very secure, however, you might want to start off with paper trades and work your way up to dealing with real money. Bear in mind that despite your best efforts, there is a chance that you will place a wager that turns out to be a losing one. However, it is advisable to take the loss as a lesson and move on.

Next, you should carry out some study. You are probably not surprised by this information, but the fact that this is one of the most typical reasons traders are unsuccessful. The phrase "laziness" is one that should never be used, but sadly, it accurately describes the behaviour of many investors. People have a tendency to put their faith in what they are told by others rather than undertaking the laborious work themselves. But putting in the necessary effort does pay off, and in the end, you will find that you have been significantly better rewarded than those who tried to wing it with the bare minimum of information.

Consider the following when determining which penny stocks are the finest ones for you to purchase: Keep in mind previous runners, hot areas, sympathy plays, and recent headlines. They should all be something you actively keep an eye on because they all play a role in the market for penny stocks. It could look like a lot of extra effort, but doing so is absolutely vital in order to keep one's skills sharp and one step ahead of the competition whenever it is required. To achieve one's goals, one must put in a significant amount of effort and also exhibit tenacity and grit. To achieve success, you will need to go above and beyond what the majority of people are ready to accomplish. Even if it is not enjoyable, doing so is really essential.

Consider the following: if you are ready to spend only another half an hour knowing as much as you can about penny stocks as well as the firm, then you are far more knowledgeable than the vast majority of traders. This provides you with leverage and an advantage that the vast majority of other individuals do not possess.

Consider the market as though you were an experienced but now-retired trader. You won't act unless you absolutely have to. Even though you are not going to be retiring anytime soon, adopting this frame of mind will help you better manoeuvre against the pent-up emotional plays that have a tendency to string along a large number of other traders. People who have the mentality of being "retired" are not going to come out of retirement to pursue a trade that is hardly valuable, even if it does have some value at all. Your time is not worth wasting on mediocre merchants. You are not aiming for a position in the minor league; rather, you are working towards acquiring the greatest possible deals.

Characteristics Of A Person Who Is Met-Averse

At this point, you may be wondering why a blockchainmetaverse is so fundamentally different from the worlds that are featured in games like The Sims and RuneScape, which are considered to be more traditional.

The metaverse that is founded on blockchain technology has three primary characteristics. In general, designers of blockchain-based metaverses have attempted to differentiate their virtual reality worlds from those of all prior incarnations, and they have placed an emphasis on the following major components:

A move away from centralised control

User governance and the value it has in the real world

Companies initially owned and exercised complete authority over all aspects of early virtual worlds. On the other hand, blockchainmetaverses have a propensity to be decentralised, with some or all of the in-world goods being constructed with the help of blockchain technology. This indicates, in essence, that blockchainmetaverses themselves have a tendency to break from the mainstream corporate structure and value extraction strategies that are typical of the gaming industry in the present day. Because of the one-of-a-kind architecture of blockchain games, more equitable engagement opportunities can be opened up for all participants. This ensures that ownership of the metaverse space is distributed fairly across everyone of the user base of the blockchain game.

When it comes to user governance, games like Decentraland, for example, use DAO models and governance tokens to help put the players themselves in command of the future road map of the game through the usage of governance mechanisms. In this approach, the metaverse environment has the potential to become much more than just a straightforward crypto game since it has the ability to transform into a whole civilization guided by its own economic and leadership models. In this way, the metaverse environment can become much more than just a simple crypto game.

Let's refer to three primary instances in order to effectively describe the real-world value component of the blockchainmetaverse:

Axie, the Infinite Axe

Both the Playground and the Network

Please be aware that nothing you read on this site should be construed as professional financial advice.

Axie, the Infinite Axe

Several months before any internet giants declared their plans to establish a metaverse, the blockchain gaming project known as Axie infinite is generally regarded as the one that first started the GameFi and metaverse movement.

When compared to the many other stunningly realistic games that are now available, Axie Infinity's visual presentation isn't quite as impressive. In point of fact, its primary focus is on characters modelled like Pokemon, which engage in combat and reproduce within the context of a simple strategic game. This non-fungible token game is not particularly complex; yet, it has already generated over 27,500 Ethereums each in trading volume on OpenSea alone, and it has over thirty thousand traders who are actively participating.

The fact that Axie provides its customers with the opportunity to earn money simply by playing the game is a significant step forward in terms of economic development, and this factor is largely responsible for the company's success. This holds true, in particular, for a great number of players in nations like the Philippines. Its popularity skyrocketed in the early part of this year as a result of the pandemic, which forced many people to lose their jobs and other sources of income.

The total number of axie NFTs that are traded may, however, be monitored, which makes it feasible to get a rough estimate of the number of people who are participating in the game. These measures demonstrate the real-world economic utility and intrinsic value of gaming non-fungible tokens (NFTs) as financial assets that may be generated on the blockchain through games and sold on the market in return for real money. Additionally, they highlight the value that gaming NFTs possess in and of themselves. Games such as Axie Infinity demonstrate why more and more tech titans are becoming interested in the metaverse concept. They effectively make it possible for everyone to modify not only how they work, earn, and spend money, but also the fundamental ways in which they live, plan, and manage their life. This is all made possible by the power of NFT gaming and, eventually, the ecosystem of the metaverse.

The Metaverse's Various Types of Business Models

The combination of decentralisation and cloud computing has resulted in a little issue with internet utilisation. LATENCY is the name given to the difficulty that it causes. The vast majority of users have, at some point or another, come across the phenomenon known as latency. When you search for a piece of information using your internet browser, there are occasions in which you will be required to wait for approximately ten seconds for the website to show or download the information that you are looking for. This happens because the data has to travel a certain distance before it can provide that conclusion, although in some instances, this is not a significant issue at all. However, if you are performing robotic surgery, this data lag or latency is something that should be taken into consideration. This is where the software development company known as FASTLY comes into play.

The technology that Fastly uses to run its edge computing architecture ushers servers and other tools closer to the location where the data is being created. The Fastly technology is capable of moving over 136 terabytes of data to approximately 27 nations in a single second. This will assist in reducing the time lag. The Metaverse will call for a large number of distributed computing systems to ensure that there is no time lag. Huge amounts of data will need to be sent in order to establish a virtual world that supports user interaction. This will be a requirement for the creation of the virtual world. Some data transfers simply cannot be completed in the absence of this company.

Nvidia ()

For a considerable amount of time, analysts have ranked Nvidia among the top stocks that investors should consider purchasing. It plays an important part in various processing chips, including those used for artificial intelligence. It has become a useful stock in the Metaverse due to the fact that it is so useful in the technologies relating to artificial intelligence. The chipset manufactured by NVDA is already making its way into numerous servers and other types of centralised computers, which are required in order to carry out complicated computations. This indicates that swiftly made use of the NVDA as well. Because it recently purchased the ARM holdings from a firm affiliated with SoftBank, it is possible that it is a stock in the Metaverse. In addition, ARM is an essential participant in the development of software and patents that make it possible for processors to be integrated into computers. Therefore, NVDA will now be able to develop its own end-to-end ecosystem with the help of this takeover. This indicates that it is capable of immediately embedding its own graphics processing unit as well as other modern processors inside systems in order to increase the power of the computer. In order for Metaverse to operate at its full potential, it will require this level of computing power.

Roblox (n.d.)

Roblox is a well-known and widely played online video game. On a daily basis, the company has 43.2 million active users that log into the game and together spend over 9.7 billion hours participating in the activity. Roblox is a platform that hosts a variety of games. It relies on third-party developers to produce a variety of material, games, and other forms of entertainment for its customers.

The company generates revenue by selling the virtual currency that customers need to use in order to gain access to the games, content, apparel, and other items such as Gucci handbags. The important thing to realise is that Roblox has, in a sense, established the groundwork for the Metaverse in its game. In the game, there is usually some kind of event going on, like a concert. Roblox might be an excellent addition to a portfolio of metaverse options.

Meta

META is the new name that Mark Zuckerberg has given to the company that Facebook is a part of. In 2014, when the firm had just purchased an Oculus virtual reality headset, this laid the groundwork for the vision of the Metaverse. However, at that time, Facebook has not precisely defined what it wanted to do about the meta, and it wasn't until relatively recently that the CEO officially announced that the company would be moving to the Metaverse. Facebook introduced a brand new Oculus application in the month of August that was dubbed horizon workrooms. Users of this VR gear have the ability to take part in gatherings represented by avatars. They are able to gaze at the computer screen as well as the keyboard. There is no question that Facebook will continue to serve as a stable platform for the expansion of the Metaverse.

Autodesk, Inc.

In the 1980s, Autodesk rose to prominence and came to be known primarily as the company that developed the first version of the AutoCAD software. Buildings, infrastructure projects, products, and other items may all be designed in 2D and 3D with the help of this programme, which is useful for architects, academicians, and designers. It is a useful piece of software for businesses, and a significant number of construction projects use it at some time during the course of their building operations.

As soon as the company realised that a large number of developers had started using the software to build and design virtual worlds for entertainment and gaming, the company made the decision to produce a suite of products that would provide 3D animation, virtual building launch, and also create augmented reality environments. This decision was made after the company observed that a large number of developers had begun using the programme. As a company that has been in the business of producing 3D designs for a very long time, Autodesk is the best option for metaverse stocks.

Providing Childcare

It is not always an easy chore for parents to take care of their children, particularly in situations when both parents are employed and must be away from the home for extended periods of time. Babysitters are the most practical option for homes with such hectic schedules.

Even if parents have plenty of free time on their hands, they could occasionally want to spend an evening together. For this reason, they might look for a young babysitter who lives in the same general area as them and hire them to look after their child overnight. You can improve your social skills while also picking up some extra cash with this fantastic opportunity. This is a terrific way to earn money because many parents are generous enough to allow babysitters access to the house refrigerator, which ensures that there is never a concern over the availability of food or water.

Check to see that the time commitment of babysitting will not interfere with your academic obligations before you agree to take on the job. It is essential for you to achieve some level of harmony with your typical routine in order to ensure that no one facet of your life is negatively impacted.

Ensure That You Make A Superb First Impression In the course of the interview. You have to first establish oneself as a trustworthy babysitter in the eyes of the homeowners. Maintain your composure in response to the questions they ask you, and demonstrate that you take responsibility seriously. One useful piece of advice is to describe the ways in which you assist your parents with the routine duties that take place in your own home.

Always make sure to get any queries you have clarified. It is possible that you will simply get to meet the parents, that you will get to know their children, or that you will meet the entire family. In any event, before the interview, you need to make sure that you have questions prepared for the parents.

When you are in the company of children, you should never leave them alone unless they are sleeping. This indicates that you ought to put aside your phone so that you are not tempted to check it, as doing so at this time would be distracting. Before you leave, check to see that they are occupied and that they are in a secure location. Then you'll be able to go in and out as soon as feasible.

● Be considerate and kind. Kids need to see you as both a friend and a leader, and hence you should babysit children who can be friends with you. Punishment goes hand in hand with being compassionate and empathetic.

When instructing youngsters, be kind to them: aid them in learning rather than just correcting their errors. Children will trust you more if you are compassionate and they will open out to you when they are in difficulty. ● Before babysitting, develop a complete list of all probable outcomes, from emergency circumstances to minor incidents. A major deal of it is contingent on staying ahead of the game.

Make a list of critical contacts with whom you can quickly connect and update if anything unexpected happens. Other family members of the children you're babysitting, neighbors, and doctors you may need to call for assistance, are all folks you should establish a list of.

Make a list of all the allergies their children have, as well as the severity, symptoms, and therapy. Remember that allergies may be triggered by several reasons, including bugs, pets, different types of food, allergies during particular seasons, drugs, creams, and more. If the child you're babysitting has an Epi-pen, know where it is and how to use it.

If you wish to prevent children from choking, be sure to ask parents what foods and toys their children are allowed to play with and eat.

When you plan for challenges ahead of time, you will be better equipped to cope with them when they come. Instead of getting irritated, you will be able to work through it more quietly.

ETFs and Mutual Funds: Which Is Better?

Due to the fact that exchange-traded funds (ETFs) and mutual funds share many similarities, a lot of people get them confused with one another. Both of them offer a diversified portfolio of funds derived from a wide variety of assets. People should have them in their portfolios because they are a fantastic method to diversify their holdings. When compared to the alternative of selecting individual stocks on your own, both of these are preferable as safer investment solutions.

Mutual funds are not passive investments; rather, they are actively managed by a fund manager who is responsible for making crucial choices on the distribution of certain assets. Purchases of mutual funds are restricted to the last few minutes of each trading day. Overall, the goal of mutual funds is to outperform the market while also providing investors with additional short-term funding options. Due to the fact that they are diverse, they continue to be viable solutions for long-term investments. If you consistently put money into a mutual fund and the fund has a positive performance history, you may end up with more wealth than you need to support yourself in retirement.

Exchange-traded funds are a better example of what we are talking about here. They are funds that are handled in a passive manner and often track a certain market index. As a consequence of this, exchange-traded funds (EFTs) have lower costs and are associated with a lower level of risk. However, there is a lower probability of achieving a significant profit. When EFT funds are used, stock transactions can take place at any time during the trading day. Because there is less potential for capital gains, individual stocks offer significant tax advantages over mutual funds. Last but not least, exchange-traded funds are simpler to invest in than mutual funds because they call for a lower initial investment. In most cases, the cost of a single share is all that is required to participate.

Metals of Valuable Worth

Rare metals that occur in their native state within the earth are classified as precious metals because of their great monetary value. They are valued more highly by societies all over the world, and individuals are more prepared to part with a greater sum of money for them than they would for basic metal. Because of their unique characteristics, precious metals are particularly well-suited for usage in the production of high-value goods such as jewelry and works of art.

Because of the precious metals' high market value, investing in them can result in growth that is both passive and sustainable over the long term. Palladium, platinum, gold, and silver are the precious metals that we will be talking about in this section. Some people keep these metals in their possession in the form of tangible objects, such as gold and silver bars, or in the shape of a variety of personal items that are fashioned from these metals. You have the option of taking this course of action and protecting your valuables by storing them in a safe or lockbox. Having a passive investing account in precious metals is still another alternative to consider. This indicates that you are able to set up something similar to an individual retirement account (IRA) that is dedicated to precious metals and let it to develop unattended over the course of time. These, just like other passive investment funds, will be handled by an industry professional, and as a result, there will be some amount of fees to pay the costs associated with having this done.

The value of precious metals is high on a global scale, and this value is not impacted by changes in the value of the currencies of specific nations. This is a remarkable feature of precious metals. Having investments in tangible assets such as gold and silver can assist mitigate the impact of losses sustained from other types of investments. For instance, the value of the dollar will decrease as a direct result of inflation, whilst the value of gold and other precious metals would continue to grow. This is a fantastic method for protecting yourself against the risk posed by your many investments.

Accounts for the investment of precious metals can be obtained from a variety of brokerage firms that are dedicated to the alternatives in question. Do some research to find out which ones have the greatest ratings, and then have a conversation with an expert about the different choices.

Intelligent Contracts

Smart contracts are a type of contract that may be made in Ethereum. They provide a solution to a significant issue, which is the question of how one can engage in a transaction via the internet when one party does not trust the other. What exactly is the mechanism that causes it?

A computerized transaction mechanism that is used to carry out the conditions of a contract is known as a "smart contract." It is standard practice for one of the parties to the contract to interpret the terms of the agreement in his or her own way. On the other hand, smart contracts are computer protocols that are designed to speed, validate, or enforce the impartial negotiation or fulfillment of a contract. These protocols can also be used to ensure that a contract is fulfilled.

As a consequence of this, smart contracts make it possible for users to exert control over their online interactions using the following means:

Offering computer assistance in the monitoring and carrying out of agreements

Bringing down the cost of carrying out an action

Contributing to the formation of relationships characterized by a greater level of trust

Non-intervention by a third party in the performance of the obligations outlined in the contract

Having both a mathematical formulation and a well outlined logic for implementation is a must.

requiring a setting in which the execution can be carried out in a completely automated manner.

Let's take a look at some of the different applications that could make use of smart contracts. To get started, you can use them to buy and sell stocks on the stock market and participate in crowdfunding initiatives. Additionally, you can use them to purchase and sell other assets. These days, getting a company's shares listed on the NYSE or NASDAQ requires a lot of companies to shell out more than $5 million. When using Blockchain, these costs are significantly reduced, and there is a possibility that they could be eliminated entirely.

It is also possible to hold a vote using smart contracts, which can help reduce the likelihood of issues such as ballot stuffing, re-voting, and improper vote counting. In addition to this, the results might be observed straight away.

The following stage, when dealing with smart contracts, is to hold an auction. Everyone will be able to take part in these auctions, which will be open to the public and entirely transparent. There will be no bribes given or corruption of any kind.

Because they provide copyright protection, smart contracts might even protect goods from being counterfeited.

It's also possible to utilize smart contracts to manage many registries at the same time. The Swedish government began experimenting with the use of Blockchain technology in 2016, with the goal of using it to keep track of all land parcels, as well as their purchase and sale.

Smart contracts may be beneficial to a wide variety of applications, including affiliate marketing programs, insurance policies, gaming and lottery operations, and transparent taxation. The benefits of smart contracts that make use of Ethereum'sBlockchain can be applied to virtually all ordinary dealings with governmental agencies.

As evidenced by the opportunities presented by intelligent contracts, this technological innovation possesses a great deal of untapped potential.

The use of smart contracts, on the other hand, is not without its drawbacks, one of which being the problem of scalability. There are limitations imposed on Bitcoin'sBlockchain. Ethereum, on the other hand, does not have any restrictions of this kind.

In conclusion, the Proof-of-Stake (PoS) mechanism used by Ethereum is a source of concern for many people. Proof of Stake (PoS) on Ethereum is analogous to the Proof of Work feature on Bitcoin, for those who aren't up to speed.

The transition of the Ethereum network from Proof-of-Work (PoW) to Proof-of-Stake (PoS) is a significant step forward in the evolution of the network. From an economic sense, remaining in PoW is incredibly irresponsible because it leads to significant inflation over time.

The creator of Ethereum, VitalikButerin, has stated that he would like to conduct a survey regarding the cryptocurrency's potential transition to provisional Proof of Work. Mining rewards for Ethereum are going to be cut in half, but there will be more options than ever before for validating transactions. When a node validates transactions (in a cryptocurrency), it will store significant amounts of the coin Ether. That is, a user is required to have a certain amount of ether in their possession in order to successfully conduct transactions. A person in this position is expected to check transactions with complete and utter honesty because they have Ether.

As you may already be aware, a PoS operates similarly to a central bank in that it stores a significant amount of cash. As a direct consequence of this, Ethereum will partially undergo a transition from decentralization to oligopoly. There will be significant "holders" that have gathered enormous sums of Ether and, as a result, have the power to conduct transactions. They plan to make money by doing things in this manner.

Long-Term Obligations And Obligations

These arrangements involve the company and the debtor entering into contracts in which they agree to pay back the money that is owed over a set amount of time, together with interest. You don't have to give too much thought to these numbers, but the trends are important to consider. If you observe that the company has been relying heavily on long term liabilities for an extended period of time, then it is possible that they are in significant trouble and are unable to make ends meet or raise needed cash from the owners they currently have or potential owners they could have in the future. Keep an eye out for any reorganization of the company's long-term debt, as the business may be sneakily searching for concessions from potential lenders.

In the event that things do not go as smoothly as they could for the company, having an excessive amount of debt can be an exceedingly perilous situation. Although it is true that the company can create more with debt financing and this will result in larger profits, it is also possible for the situation to work in the opposite direction. The last thing a value investor wants to do is put their money into a questionable firm that has a lot of debt because it would be a terrible idea.

Equity held by the owners

The stock held by the company's owners is vitally necessary for the continued existence of the business. Having said that, there isn't much for you to look at in this area. When it comes to owners' equity, there are only a few things you should be concerned with, and we are going to keep to those:

The total amount of money that the owners of a firm, also known as shareholders, have contributed to the business is referred to as paid-in capital. The capital that was paid in at the time of initial stock sales, also known as company stock sales, is included in the total paid-in capital. You don't need to pay any attention to this because it has absolutely nothing to do with the price or the value of the market.

The gains that a firm produced during prior operating periods that were then reinvested or otherwise put back into the business are referred to as the company's retained earnings. It is up to the management to decide whether or not they should make a payout, despite the fact that the company has the potential to be profitable, which means that you can also be profitable as an investor. In most cases, the managers would prefer to invest those sums in order to generate even higher returns, and the investors are more than glad to let them retain the earnings.

When it comes to investing, most people don't mind seeing exceptionally large retained earnings as long as the company is doing well. It all comes down to efficiently distributing the available resources. The crux of the matter is that it will be to everyone's advantage to keep the gains rather than distribute them. There is no harm in allowing your profits to grow even further.

If the dividend policy is fair, in the sense that the owners get to enjoy some of the rewards of their investment, then retained earnings is a fantastic thing. However, this is only the case if the dividend policy is reasonable. On the other hand, you need to be very wary about a drop in retained earnings or, even worse, negative retained earnings. Both of these scenarios are quite problematic. This is going to cause problems. It could suggest that the assets are deteriorating at a rate that is considerably quicker than was anticipated in the past, that there is excessive inflation in the price at which the stock is being offered, that there is an excessive amount of debt, or that all three of these factors are present. To abbreviate the long story: Run.

In principle, the book value of the company is the same thing as the owners' equity. It is the difference between the face value liabilities and assets that have been recorded (with some wiggle room). When it comes to a company's book value, value investors consider three distinct metrics:

• Book value is calculated by subtracting liabilities from total book assets, also known as owners' equity.

The basic definition of tangible book value is the overall book value reduced by some or all of the intangible assets.

The recorded book value is divided by the total number of common shares that are currently in circulation to arrive at the book value per share.

You can frequently find these measurements in papers, journals, and other publications related to investing; nevertheless, you need to be careful because these phrases are occasionally used interchangeably with one another. A correct evaluation of book value requires that you not obsess over the total book value; if you do, you risk becoming frustrated while attempting to go over it using the information that is given to you. Instead, you ought to focus on the shifts and tendencies that have occurred. When compared to the activities of the business, the book value should be considered. The next step is to evaluate the company's book value in relation to that of the company's competitors and the industry as a whole.

When it comes to booking value, it essentially refers to the amount of money that the investors keep or invest in the company. On the other hand, what the investors can receive out of the company is what constitutes the company's intrinsic worth. The book value of the company is of the utmost significance when attempting to ascertain the true value of the company. However, there is one more aspect of its intrinsic value that is very important, and that is the investor's potential to earn a net present income stream as well as a net future income stream from the company. This is a very important part of its value.

In conclusion, keep in mind the tax burden as well as the cost of pursuing immediate profits as opposed to retaining your investment for a period of one year. This is a significant problem for people who are on the lower rungs of the income ladder and for people who get help from the government. You should be aware that any profit that is claimed within a year of the date on which the investment was made needs to be included as income on your most recent tax filings. This will result in a different amount of taxable income, and it may also cause you to lose eligibility for certain benefits. Always verify whether or not it makes more sense financially for you to claim for the short term capital gains tax by either checking online or consulting with a professional accountant. You can do either of these things. In the beginning, it was far more prudent for me to pay the higher tax penalty; however, when my financial situation improved, it became abundantly evident that the long term capital gains tax was significantly more advantageous.

The Best Digital Currencies Available For Investment On The Market Today

What do you think of this book so far? In that case, I'd be really grateful if you could write a brief review of the book on Amazon; your feedback would mean a great deal to me. I am grateful.

Cryptocurrencies are almost always intended to be free from manipulation and control by governments; yet, as their popularity has increased, the essential component of the sector has come under assault.

Alternate cryptocurrencies, sometimes known as "shitcoins," are digital currencies that were formed in the wake of Bit coin. These cryptocurrencies have frequently attempted to portray themselves as updated or improved versions of Bit coin, despite the fact that they are not.

Although some of these currencies may contain remarkable qualities that Bit coin does not possess, no other currency has yet reached the same degree of security that Bit coin's networks have achieved, which is a significant achievement. While some of these currencies may possess exceptional properties that Bit coin does not possess, no alternative currency has yet achieved the same level of security.

Uses of crypto currency as Examples

The utilization of crypto currencies has experienced meteoric growth ever since the launch of Bit coin. Even while the exact number of active currencies is subject to change and the prices of individual currencies are subject to extreme swings, the total market value of all active crypto currencies is normally on the rise. This is despite the fact that the prices of individual currencies are subject to extreme swings.

On the market, hundreds of different crypto currencies are exchanged for one another every second.

The crypto currencies that are listed below are notable for a number of reasons, including their widespread adoption, strong user activity, and reasonably substantial market capitalization (in most cases, greater than $10 million; although, prices are subject to change):

1. The cryptocurrency bit coin

Bit coin is the crypto currency that is used the most all around the world, and its widespread adoption is largely attributed with popularizing the cryptocurrency movement. Prior to 2011, the only cryptocurrency that could be used to make an investment was bit coin. Altcoins, also known as alternative coins, first came into being as a response to the shortcomings of Bit Coin; hence, this is how they came to be known (as alternatives to Bit Coin). They improved the design of Bit Coin in a multitude of aspects, including speed, security, obscurity, and a few other things as well. At the moment, there is a diverse range of crypto currencies available, as well as a multitude of other applications for the blockchain technology. One of the earliest alternative cryptocurrencies to ever exist was called Lit Coin.

Establish Objectives

It is my hope that it is becoming increasingly obvious that the concept of abundance has a great deal to do with how one thinks, and not just with numbers and bank balances. If you want to become wealthy, you should be motivated by something that relentlessly drives you toward growth. This should be a goal that will transform you in such a way that will make you happy. The pursuit of our goals employs a unique strategy for assisting us in overcoming challenges. Assuming you have a clear understanding of what it is that you genuinely require, you will find out a way to acquire it.

Recall your time spent in medical school, graduate school, or even elementary school. What were you hoping to accomplish at that time and place? to participate in activities that go from nightfall till dawn, to successfully complete tests, and to endure the occasional humiliation at the hands of trainers and mentors? No. The goal was to graduate from college, become a specialist in the field, or become a legal counselor. That equipped you with the fortitude to fight on and persevere through all challenges in order to obtain what you required. That is the power that comes from having a goal.

When my son was in high school, he provided me with one of the most compelling examples of effective objective setting that I've ever seen. He competed in grappling. It was something he took tremendous pride in, and he excelled at it. Every day, he would get up well before six in the morning to train with his best friend before school, and then he would practice again once school was over. Those of you who are unfamiliar with wrestling should know that it is a challenging sport that pits you against the subsequent competitor in a mano a mano match. In the event that you are unsuccessful, there is no one to blame. The preparation is difficult, and as a result, many people drop out.

Before the beginning of his regular season, he confidently predicted that he would end up as the state champion. There are those who would refer to this as a "major, hairy, audacious objective" (BHAG). It was extremely brazen in view of the fact that there was no evidence to suggest that he was even marginally adequate. Up until that point, all I could do was be content with the fact that he possessed the mental fortitude to continue playing the game.

His dedication paid off, as he only dropped one match throughout the entire year, and it was to the grappler with the highest level in the state of Texas. This occurred just at the beginning of the season, and after the match, the contradicting mentor and grappler were being really pretentious when he approached them for the customary victory handshake. This had a significant impact on him. Even though he had already achieved his primary objective, which was to win state, he knew that he needed one more opportunity to compete against that opponent.

During the course of that year, he developed the habit of buckling down each day and never deviating from his preparation in any way. As we got closer to the state tournament, he was ranked number two, and the wrestler who had been responsible for his most significant defeat was in the number one spot. My child had been experiencing unexplainable exhaustion during the entirety of the school year, but he chalked it up to nervousness on his part. (On further investigation, we found out that he had mononucleosis.) He never stopped preparing and never allowed himself to become distracted.

In the end, the two competitors came face to face. It was a truly magnificent contest. My child was somewhere around a point and in a terrible position with eight seconds remaining to go, looking a lot like he was making a beeline for one more runner up finish. Suddenly, he came up with a maneuver that provided him dual focuses on the situation. When the bell rang, he was crowned champion of the state.

Later, when he was confronted with the question of what he had been considering at that time, he responded, "Continue to wrestle." I was given the order to continue fighting until the final whistle blew.

My child never stopped because he had a goal to attain, and he wouldn't let anything go in the way of achieving that goal, not even a sickness that would keep the vast majority of people confined to bed. At this point in time, if things get challenging in medicine or business, his example of commitment and consistency gives me the solidarity to keep battling.

Due care and attention

After you have made an offer on a house, it has been acknowledged, and you have come to an agreement with the seller, the time has come for you to begin your investigation into the matter. You are able to accomplish some of this prior to making a deal; however, depending on your market, time is typically of the essence in most situations. In addition, you will have to spend money and time finishing research on properties on which you and the vendors might not be able to come to an agreement.

Your loan specialist or intermediary will hire an appraiser to verify that the property is valued at the amount necessary to cover the cost of doing business. Your financial specialist will also require that a title report be completed in order to ensure that the title is clear of any liens. You need to perform a careful examination of this in order to look for any unexpected liens or easements.

You ought to get in touch with a home monitor so that they can direct a comprehensive search of the property. You should make every effort to be present throughout the evaluation. Your real estate agent ought to give you the option of requesting that they provide you with a list of qualified professionals from which you can make your selection.

In addition to this, you should seriously consider carrying out an ecological survey on both the home and the surrounding land. The results of this inspection will tell you whether or not there is asbestos, lead, or any other potentially hazardous poisons present. These can quickly become expensive, so you will simply need to decide whether or not it is worthwhile to finish despite the cost.

Following receipt of the auditor's report detailing the discrepancies, you may have the option to go back to the dealer and request that things be straightened out. In the event that the property is found in a solid economically constrained market, the vendor may refuse, and in the event that you and the vendor are unable to come to an agreement, you may choose to back out of the agreement and place the property back on the market. However, regardless of the state of the market, the home inspection needs to be carried out on a regular basis. After purchasing and remodeling a couple hundred homes, I started conducting these investigations on my own. Despite my best efforts, I was unable to avoid making this crucial advance in any of my earlier purchases. Due to the fact that the market is weak, you may be successful in returning to the dealer and expecting them to either address the issues or provide you with a price reduction if you buy a home in a market that is open to the public. This makes the inspections particularly important in such a market because virtually every home inspection finds various things that need to be amended. Even though you have to pay for the inspection with cash that you already have, the cost is typically more than made up for by the things that the vendor fixes for you.

Comparison of Loan Brokers and Direct Lenders

You will need to make a decision regarding whether you will work with an advance representative or an immediate moneylender before you even begin your search for a property. Both have their positive and negative aspects to consider.

Your credit agent will make contact with a large number of loan specialists (sometimes as many as 300), and they will search for the most advantageous interest rate and terms on your behalf. They will also act as a go-between for you and help you fix any issues that arise with your application without causing you to lose the arrangement. The most important thing is that you, as the client, are responsible for paying the specialist and that they work for you. The fact that you have to pay them is a drawback. To complete the transaction, they will typically deduct between one half point and one full point (as a percentage of the total advance amount). This charge can frequently be remembered for the credit installment, and when combined with the limited rate that they get, their expense may become less significant than it otherwise would be. You need to make it crystal clear to your agent right away that you want a credit with "no points or start cost," and then they will determine your rates based on whether or not you remember the cost of the advance payment.

On the other hand, a direct lender, such as a local bank or an online company like Rocket Mortgage or Quicken Loans, does not charge a significant amount for an origination fee, if they charge one at all. In spite of this, there is a possibility that the cost of financing will be slightly higher if you shop around (something that is the responsibility of an intermediary) than if you do not. Because they are employed by the moneylender, the nearby bank won't be able to assist you if you run into problems while the advance is being processed because they are prohibited from doing so by their employer. Working openly and honestly with a moneylender allows you to establish a standing, which is one of the benefits of this arrangement. If you end up doing many credits through one moneylender and consistently pay on schedule, they will turn out to be more able to help you with future advances and will assist you with developing your land speculation portfolio. If you pay on schedule, however, they will not be able to help you with developing your land speculation portfolio.

The process of lending is based on numbers, but individual connections can have a significant bearing on the outcome at the community level. Developing a personal relationship with a credit official at a local bank is a fantastic idea if you intend to buy a series of investment properties, which is something that you should definitely consider doing because I hope that you will.

Conclusion

You are now familiar with the methods that are required to generate significant profits from investments over both the short and the long term. You are aware of the tax burden as well as the strategies that experienced traders use to generate profits in the markets. You are aware that the time commitment is minimal, and that the only thing necessary to get started is to begin making investments. You are also aware of the many benefits that come with investing, as well as the fact that you should get started as soon as you possibly can. Even if you are having trouble saving money and investing at the moment, it is still in your best interest to begin doing so because the potential rewards are so substantial.

The next thing you need to do is establish your investment pool and look for an investment that not only satisfies your needs for producing income but is also appropriate for the amount of money you have available to work with. The two areas that I would recommend beginning with first and foremost are dividend stocks and peer-to-peer lending. You'll start receiving interest payments from peer-to-peer lending within the first thirty days, and dividend stocks will send you checks periodically throughout the year. Simply consult the recommendations made by Warren Buffett, the value investor on whose principles the ideas presented in this book are based, to obtain a list of excellent dividend stocks. It has only been a few short years since I first started investing, but in that time, the stock market investments that I have made have all been based on the advice that Warren has given me, and they have shown to be quite profitable.